FAVOURITE CHICKEN RECIPES

*Soups, Grills
Pies, Casseroles
and Supper Dishes*

*with illustrations by
Helen Allingham RWS*

SALMON

Index

Cover pictures: *front:* At the Farm Gate *by Henry King*
back: High Summer *by Berenger Benger*
Printed and Published by J. Salmon Ltd., Sevenoaks, England ©

Lemon Chicken

A tangy casseroled chicken served with a rich sauce; ideal for a special occasion.

4 lb chicken	**3 peppercorns**
1 large lemon	**Salt and pepper**
8 oz small onions, peeled	**4 oz button mushrooms, halved**
and left whole	**2 oz butter**
8 oz carrots, sliced thickly	**1 egg**
2-3 sticks celery, sliced thickly	**4 tablespoons cream**
3 bay leaves	**¼ pint sherry**

4 oz blanched almonds

Set oven to 300°F or Mark 2. Put the chicken in a casserole dish. Squeeze the lemon juice over the bird and put the lemon halves (pips removed) in the cavity. Add the vegetables, bayleaves and peppercorns and season. Cover with water and bring to the boil. Cover, put in the oven and cook for about 1 to 1½ hours until the chicken is tender. Transfer the chicken to a serving dish, surround with the drained vegetables and keep warm. Reserve the stock. Fry the mushrooms in the butter. Beat the egg and the cream together in a saucepan, gradually add ½ pint of the reserved stock, stirring continually, and heat gently until thick and smooth. Add the mushrooms, sherry and almonds to the hot sauce and pour around the chicken. Serves 4 to 6.

Chicken Kedgeree

Originally made with fish and served at breakfast, chicken kedgeree makes a supper dish accompanied with salad.

12 oz cooked chicken, diced	**1 onion, finely chopped**
6 oz Patna rice	**2 hard boiled eggs**
A small walnut of butter	**2 tablespoons cream**
½ teaspoon salt	**Salt and pepper**
1 pint water	**Chopped fresh parsley**
2 oz butter	**to garnish**

Melt the walnut of butter in a saucepan, pour in the rice and stir to coat the grains. Then add the water with ½ teaspoon of salt, bring to the boil, cover and simmer very gently until all the water is absorbed; about 20 to 25 minutes. Meanwhile, melt some of the 2 oz of butter in a frying pan and fry the onion until soft and transparent. Chop up the egg whites and mash the yolks separately with a fork. When the rice is cooked, stir into it the chicken pieces, the onion, egg whites, the remainder of the butter and the cream and season. Transfer to a warmed serving dish and garnish with the egg yolk and chopped parsley. Serves 4.

Cheesy Chicken Pie

This tasty pie is an excellent way of using up cold roast chicken.

¾-1 lb cooked chicken, diced	¼ pint dry cider
1 oz butter	1 small onion, finely diced
1 oz flour	4 oz Cheddar cheese, grated
½ pint milk	Salt and pepper

8 oz shortcrust pastry

Set oven to 400°F or Mark 6. Melt the butter in a large frying pan and add the flour. Cook for 2 to 3 minutes, stirring all the time. Remove from the heat and stir in the milk and cider, a little at a time. Return to the heat and continue stirring until the sauce thickens. Add the onion and cook for 5 minutes. Next add the cheese and lastly the chicken and seasoning. Transfer the mixture into a pie dish. Roll out the pastry on a lightly floured surface and use to cover the dish. Trim and decorate with the pastry trimmings. Cook for approximately 30 minutes, until the pastry is golden in colour. Serves 4.

Chicken Balls

Chicken rissoles cooked in stock and served with a creamy sauce.

1 lb raw chicken, minced	*To thicken:*
1 egg, beaten	**1 oz butter, softened**
3 tablespoons fresh white	**1 oz flour**
breadcrumbs	**2-3 tablespoons cream**
Salt and pepper	*To garnish:*
3 tablespoons cream	**Chopped fresh parsley**
1 pint chicken stock	**Lemon quarters**

Blend the minced chicken with the egg and breadcrumbs, season well and beat in the cream, gradually. Form into balls with floured hands. Heat the stock in a large saucepan and cook the balls for 10 to 12 minutes. Lift out, set aside on a serving dish and keep warm. Mix the butter and flour together in a pan over a low heat to make a roux, stir in the stock gradually, bring to the boil and cook until thickened. Remove from the heat and stir in the cream. Pour the sauce over the balls and serve hot, garnished with parsley and lemon quarters. Serves 4.

Curried Chicken

A tasty curry which can be adjusted from mild to hot to suit all tastes.

1 lb raw chicken meat, diced	½ teaspoon ground ginger
2 oz butter	2 teaspoons sugar
2 onions, chopped	Salt and pepper
1 apple, peeled, cored and roughly chopped	¾ pint chicken stock
1 tablespoon curry powder (according to taste)	1 teaspoon curry paste (optional)
1 tablespoon flour	1 stick celery, chopped
½ teaspoon turmeric	2 tablespoons sultanas or raisins
	1 dessertspoon chutney (as available)
	1 dessertspoon lemon juice

Heat the butter in a large saucepan and fry the onion and apple until soft. Stir in the curry powder and flour and cook for 2 to 3 minutes. Stir in the spices and sugar, season well, stir in the stock and bring gradually to the boil. Add the chicken pieces and all the other ingredients, lower the heat, cover the pan and simmer gently for about 1 hour or until the meat is tender. If the mixture seems a little thick, add water as appropriate. Stir occasionally to prevent sticking. Serve with more chutney and boiled rice or creamed potatoes. Serves 4.

By a Devonshire Co

Chicken Galantine

Galantine is a dish said to date back to Roman days. This recipe can be eaten cold with salad or hot with vegetables.

1 lb chicken breasts	¼ pint double cream
1 lb cooked ham	Salt and black pepper
4 oz fresh white breadcrumbs	¼ teaspoon grated nutmeg
2 tablespoons chopped fresh parsley	8 rashers streaky bacon, lightly stretched
2 eggs	Parsley sprigs to garnish

Set oven to 375°F or Mark 5. Lightly butter a 2 lb loaf tin. Mince together the chicken and ham, then stir in the breadcrumbs and parsley. Beat the eggs together with the cream, add seasoning and grated nutmeg and stir into the chicken/ham mixture until well combined. Line the loaf tin with the bacon rashers, overlapping them slightly. Then spoon in the chicken/ham mixture, press down lightly and smooth over the top. Wrap over any protruding bacon rasher ends. Cover with buttered greaseproof paper and kitchen foil and tie down. Stand in a '*bain marie*' and cook for 1 to 1¼ hours, removing the foil and greaseproof paper for the final 15 minutes. Cool slightly in the tin, then turn out and cool completely. Serve garnished with parsley and with salad and boiled potatoes. Alternatively, serve hot with boiled potatoes, carrots and peas. Serves 4 to 6.

Sweet and Sour Chicken

A simple way of producing a light and tasty dish accompanied with rice or noodles.

12 oz cooked chicken, diced	**2–3 sticks celery, chopped**
½ pint white wine or cider	**1 heaped tablespoon sugar**
4 large tomatoes, sliced	**1 teaspoon capers**
Salt and pepper	

Put the wine, tomato slices, celery, sugar and capers into a saucepan and season. Bring to the boil and simmer for about 30 minutes. Add the chicken pieces and continue simmering for about 20 minutes more, until the chicken is well heated through. Serve on a bed of boiled rice, couscous or noodles. Serves 4.

Chicken Tomato Soup

A good way of turning a left-over roast or boiled chicken into tasty, home made soup.

1 chicken carcase	**1 tablespoon cornflour**
Cooked chicken, chopped	**¼ pint water**
12 oz tomatoes	**Salt and pepper**
2 pints chicken stock	**4 tablespoons cream**

Remove all the residual meat from the left-over chicken and set aside. Put the carcase, tomatoes and stock into a large saucepan, bring to the boil and simmer, covered, for 1 hour. Strain well into a clean saucepan to remove the bones and tomato skins and pips, and add the reserved chopped chicken. Blend the cornflour with the water and stir in. Bring to the boil and boil, uncovered, for 10 minutes. Remove from the heat, season, stir in the cream and serve. Serves 4

Asparagus with Chicken

A delicious way of using up cooked chicken, served in an asparagus sauce.

1 tin asparagus spears, approx. 10 oz
1 pint chicken stock
3 oz butter
3 oz flour

¼ pint single cream
Lemon juice
1 lb cooked chicken meat, chopped
2 hard boiled eggs

Salt and black pepper

In a saucepan, gently heat the asparagus in the liquor from the tin. Drain the liquor from the asparagus and make up to 1¼ pints with the stock. Melt the butter in a pan, add the flour and cook for one minute. Add the stock gradually, stirring constantly. Add the cream, season and add lemon juice to taste. Setting aside a few asparagus spears for decoration, chop the rest with the chicken meat, add one chopped hard boiled egg and stir into the sauce; warm through but do not boil. Put the mixture into a hot shallow dish. Arrange the remaining asparagus spears on the mixture, radiating from the centre of the dish with slices of hard boiled egg in between. Serve with triangles of crisply fried bread for high tea, or with creamed potatoes and vegetables as a main dish. Serves 4.

Chicken Mousse

A delicious starter or a light luncheon dish.

1 level tablespoon powdered
   gelatine
2½ fl oz hot water
12 oz cooked chicken, minced
1 level teaspoon salt
Pinch cayenne pepper

2 tablespoons finely chopped
   green pepper
1 tablespoon chopped fresh parsley
¼ pint thick cream
Lettuce leaves and stuffed olives
   to garnish

Dissolve the gelatine in the hot water. In a bowl, mix together the minced chicken, salt, cayenne, chopped pepper and parsley and add the dissolved gelatine. Whip the cream and fold into the chicken mixture. Take a suitable size mould, either plain or decorated, wet with cold water and spoon in the mixture. Allow to cool and then put into the refrigerator to chill thoroughly. Turn out on to a bed of lettuce leaves on a serving dish and garnish with sliced stuffed olives; or serve with a salad. Serves 4 to 6.

Chicken in Red Wine

A quick and easy version of 'coq au vin'.

4 chicken joints	4 oz small button mushrooms
1 oz butter	2–3 rashers bacon, diced
1 tablespoon oil	¾ oz flour
12–18 little onions (cocktail onions will do)	¾ pint red wine
	Salt and pepper

Set oven to 375°F or Mark 5. Heat the butter and oil in a frying pan and fry the chicken joints on both sides until browned. Transfer to a casserole dish and keep warm in the oven. In the remaining fat (adding more if needed) fry the onions until browned (drain bottled onions well). Add the mushrooms and diced bacon and fry for 2 to 3 minutes more. Add to the chicken. Stir the flour into the remaining fat, gradually stir in the wine, bring to the boil and cook to a smooth sauce. Pour over the chicken, put in the oven and cook for about 30 minutes until the chicken is tender. Serves 4.

Skirlie Stuffed Chicken

A versatile Scottish dish. Skirlie was often eaten instead of meat, especially when times were hard. Here it makes a delicious stuffing to go with roast chicken.

3–3½ lb chicken with the giblets
4 oz medium or coarse oatmeal
1 medium onion, chopped
2 oz shredded suet or 2 oz dripping
Salt and pepper
Dried mixed herbs
A little butter for basting

Set oven to 350°F or Mark 4. Remove the giblets and boil in water with a chicken stock cube to make the gravy. Rinse, wipe and dry the chicken well. Put the oatmeal, onion and the suet or dripping into a bowl. Add salt, pepper and herbs to taste. Mix well with a fork. Stuff the chicken, but take care not to overfill the cavity as the oatmeal swells when cooked. Place the chicken in a roasting tin, spread a little butter over the breast and legs and roast for about 20 minutes to the pound and possibly 20 minutes over, depending on the bird. Serve with roast potatoes and fresh vegetables. Serves 4.

Chicken Florentine

A spinach base, baked chicken dish with a cheesy topping.

4 chicken breasts	Salt and pepper
2 oz butter or oil	2 tablespoons fresh white
1 lb spinach	breadcrumbs
4 tablespoons cream or milk	2 tablespoons grated hard cheese

Set oven to 375°F or Mark 5. Fry the chicken breasts in the butter or oil until just golden. Meanwhile, cook the spinach, strain and press out the water and mix with the cream. Season. Arrange the spinach mixture in the bottom of an ovenproof dish. Place the partially cooked chicken breasts on top and sprinkle over the breadcrumbs and grated cheese. Pour any oil or butter remaining in the pan over the topping and bake for about 30 minutes until cooked through and browned on top. Serves 4.

Chicken Hash

A fried cake of chicken and mashed potato; an easy way to use up left-overs for breakfast or supper.

12 oz cooked chicken	**1 tablespoon oil**
12 oz mashed potato	**¼ pint chicken stock**
3 onions, thinly sliced	**Salt and pepper**
1 oz butter	**Chopped fresh parsley to garnish**

Use left-over mashed potato, if available or boil sufficient potatoes in salted water and mash. Cut the chicken into tiny pieces and mix with the mashed potato. Slice the onions very thinly. Heat the butter and oil in a large frying pan and fry the onions until softened. Moisten the chicken/potato mix with sufficient stock to produce the consistency of thick cream and season very well. Add to the onions in the pan, mix well together and smooth flat. Fry over a good heat until the bottom is really crisp and brown and well heated right through. Fold over like an omelette, slide on to a hot serving dish and garnish with parsley. Serves 4.

Chicken and Leek Casserole

A simple casserole dish, thickened with oatmeal and flavoured with yeast extract.

6 chicken breasts
2 tablespoons wholemeal flour
2 tablespoons porridge oats
1 tablespoon oil
2 medium onions, sliced

2 medium leeks, chopped
2 rashers streaky bacon, chopped
6 oz mushrooms, sliced
2 teaspoons yeast extract
Salt and pepper

Set oven to 350°F or Mark 4. Mix the flour and oatmeal together in a large bowl and season well. Coat the chicken breasts evenly with this mixture. Heat the oil in a large flameproof casserole and brown the breasts on both sides. Remove and set aside in the bowl of flour mixture. Re-heat the oil, adding a little extra if necessary, and cook the onions, leeks, bacon and mushrooms, covered, over a medium heat for 5 minutes, stirring to prevent browning too much. Replace the breasts in the casserole with the remaining flour mixture, stir well, add the yeast extract and sufficient water to cover the chicken. Stir, bring to the boil, cover and cook in the oven for about 1½ hours, until the chicken is tender. Alternatively, simmer on top of the stove for about 1½ hours. Serves 6.

Chicken Parcels

The light, fresh taste of the apple stuffing makes these chicken pasties moist and appetising.

2 chicken breasts
2 oz butter
1 onion, finely chopped
1 small eating apple (e.g. Cox)
peeled, cored and finely chopped
2 oz fresh white breadcrumbs

Grated rind of ½ lemon
Salt and black pepper
1 egg, beaten
8 oz to 12 oz shortcrust pastry
(depending on size of chicken breasts)
A little beaten egg to glaze

Set oven to 400°F or Mark 6. Grease a baking tray. Cut a slit in the side of each breast to form a pocket. Melt 1 oz of the butter in a frying pan and lightly fry the breasts on both sides for about one minute to seal. Mix the onion and apple together. Melt the remaining butter in a saucepan and add the onion/apple mixture. Cover and cook over a very low heat until the onion and apple are soft. Mix together the onion/apple mixture, breadcrumbs, lemon rind and seasoning, then bind with the beaten egg. Stuff the pockets in the chicken breasts with the mixture. Roll out the pastry on a lightly floured surface. Divide in half and wrap up the breasts to form parcels, sealing well. Decorate with trimmings. Brush with milk or beaten egg to glaze and place on the baking tray. Cook for about 30 minutes or until the pastry is golden brown. Transfer to a wire rack to cool and serve cold. Serves 2.

Honeyed Chicken and Peaches

Roast chicken cooked with peaches and coated with a honey butter sauce.

3–3½ lb chicken	**8 pieces cinnamon stick**
A good knob of butter	**2 tablespoons honey**
8 canned peach halves,	**2 oz butter**
well drained	**1½ oz blanched almonds**
16 cloves	**Watercress to garnish**

Set oven to 375°F or Mark 5. Wash and dry the chicken, put a good knob of butter inside and place in a large roasting tin. Stick 2 cloves in each peach half, put a piece of cinnamon stick in the centre of each and arrange, cut side up, around the bird in the tin. Melt the honey and 2 oz butter together in a pan and pour over the chicken and peach halves. Cover with a piece of greaseproof paper, put into the oven and roast for 30 minutes. Remove the paper and sprinkle the almonds into the pan. Return to the oven for about a further 45 minutes, basting occasionally. When cooked, turn out on to a hot dish and serve, garnished with watercress. Make a gravy with some water added to the pan juices with a chicken stock cube, boil, thicken and serve. Serves 4.

Chicken, Pork and Herb Pie

This tasty pie is a meal in itself and goes well with a crisp green salad.

For Pastry: **1½ lb flour**	**2 teaspoons salt**	**4 oz lard**	**2 oz butter**	**10 fl oz water**

For Filling:

1 lb chicken (breast or thigh meat), sliced	**½ teaspoon ground mace**	**Salt and pepper**
	¼ teaspoon grated nutmeg	**1 egg, beaten**
1 lb pork fillet, sliced	**1 tablespoon chopped thyme**	**2 teaspoons gelatine, powdered**
1 onion, chopped	**½ tablespoon chopped sage**	
	3 tablespoons chopped parsley	**10 fl oz hot chicken stock**

Set oven to 400°F or Mark 6. Grease a deep, 8 inch round cake tin, with a removable base. Sift the flour and salt into a bowl and make a well. Heat the lard, butter and water in a pan and bring to the boil. Pour into the flour and mix to a soft dough. Turn out on a floured surface and knead until smooth. Set aside a quarter of the dough, covered, in a warm place and line the tin. Layer the chicken and pork in the pastry case, scattering the layers with the herbs and season with salt and pepper. Roll out the reserved pastry and cover the pie, dampening the edges to seal. Decorate and cut a steam hole. Brush with beaten egg. Bake for 30 minutes. Brush again with egg, reduce temperature to 325°F or Mark 3 and bake for another 45 minutes until golden brown. Dissolve the gelatine in the hot stock, season to taste and, as the pie cools, pour the stock into the steam hole using a small funnel. Chill overnight. Serves 6.

Chicken Fritters

These deep fried cakes can have finely chopped ham or cheese included in the filling for added flavour.

12 oz–1 lb cooked chicken, minced	**A little chopped chives**
	2 tablespoons cream
A little chopped parsley	**Flour for dusting**

For Sauce:

1 oz butter	**¼ pint milk**
1 oz flour	**Salt and pepper**

For Batter:

2 oz flour	**1 egg**
Pinch of salt	**2½ fl oz milk**

First make a white sauce. Melt the butter in a saucepan, stir in the flour and gradually beat in the milk over a low heat until it thickens into a smooth sauce. Season. Add the minced chicken, parsley, chives and cream and stir together. Allow to cool. When cool, form into round flat cakes and dust with flour. Make the batter by beating together in a bowl the flour, salt, egg and milk. Heat a pan of oil for deep frying. Dip the cakes into the batter, lower into the fat and cook until crisp and golden brown. Drain on kitchen paper, keep warm and serve with a salad. Serves 4.

Chicken and Potato Pie

A lighter variation of the more usual lamb or beef based shepherd's or cottage pies.

8 oz cooked chicken, cut into small pieces	1 tablespoon oil
8 oz potatoes, mashed	1 oz flour
1 onion, chopped	½ pint chicken stock
	1 dessertspoon tomato purée
Salt and pepper	

Set oven to 400°F or Mark 6. Put the potatoes on to boil in salted water. Meanwhile heat the oil in a saucepan, add the onion and fry until softened. Stir in the flour and cook for a minute or two longer. Gradually stir in the stock and the tomato purée, bring to the boil and boil for 2 to 3 minutes to thicken. Add the cooked chicken to the sauce, mix together and pour into an ovenproof dish. Mash the cooked potatoes with a little milk, season well, spread over the chicken mix and level out evenly with a fork. Put in the oven long enough to brown the potato topping, or brown under a hot grill. Serve with a green vegetable. Serves 4.

If it is desired to use uncooked chicken, first fry the chicken pieces in the pan until cooked through. Remove and set aside and continue as the recipe.

Grilled Chicken Breasts

A simple and quick-to-make herby grilled chicken dish.

4 chicken breasts, skinned	**1 tablespoon chopped parsley**
Grated rind and juice of one lemon	**1 tablespoon chopped thyme**
½ tablespoon chopped sage	**8 rashers streaky bacon**

Set the grill to hot. Flatten the chicken breasts with a wet knife and cut in half lengthways. Brush the chicken pieces with lemon juice. Mix together all the herbs and sprinkle each piece of chicken with the herbs and lemon rind. Wrap a rasher of streaky bacon around each piece of chicken and grill until cooked. Serve two pieces of chicken to each person with roast or sauté potatoes and a green vegetable. Serves 4.

Cocky Leeky Soup

A chicken and leek soup that is a traditional Scottish speciality.

1 small chicken with the giblets (2½–3 lb)	6 leeks, cut into pieces one inch long
3 pints water	1 small carrot, grated
1 onion, chopped	Salt and pepper
2 oz long grain rice	1 tablespoon chopped parsley

Place the chicken, giblets and onion in a large saucepan. Add the water and bring to the boil. Cover and simmer for 1½ hours until the chicken is tender. Remove from the heat and skim off any white scum. Take out the giblets and discard. Take out the chicken and strip the meat from the bones. Discard the skin and bones. Return the meat to the stock. Add the rice, leeks and grated carrot. Bring back to the boil, cover and simmer for a further 30 minutes. Season with salt and pepper to taste. Add the parsley before serving. Serves 6 to 8.

Chicken Pudding

A steamed chicken suet pudding.

8 oz self raising flour	**4 rashers bacon, diced**
½ teaspoon salt	**4 oz button mushrooms,**
4 oz shredded suet	**halved or sliced**
4 chicken joints	**Chicken stock**
1 onion, chopped	**Salt and pepper**

Grease a 2 pint pudding basin. Sift the flour and salt into a bowl and combine the suet. Mix with just sufficient cold water to form a workable but not sticky dough. Roll out on a lightly floured surface and use three-quarters of the pastry to line the pudding basin. Arrange the chicken joints in the basin with the onion, bacon and mushrooms, season well, and add about a cupful of stock. Cover with a pastry lid, moistening the edges and seal well. Cover and seal with kitchen foil and steam for about 4 hours, topping up the water as necessary. Use the remaining stock to make a gravy, thickened with a little cornflour. Serves 4.

Cheesy Chicken Casserole

Chicken portions first roasted, then covered with a rich cheese sauce and browned.

4 chicken portions	**¼ pint dry cider**
2 oz butter	**4 oz Cheddar cheese, grated**
1 medium onion, diced	**1 level teaspoon made**
1 oz flour	**English mustard**
¾ pint milk	**Salt and pepper**

Set oven to 350°F or Mark 4. Melt half the butter in a frying pan and lightly brown the chicken portions. Transfer to a casserole dish and roast in the oven for approximately 1 hour until cooked through. Prepare the sauce by melting the remaining 1 oz butter in a saucepan and gently cooking the onion until soft and transparent. Stir in the flour and cook gently for 2 to 3 minutes, stirring all the time. Remove the pan from the heat and gradually stir in all the milk and cider. Return to the heat and bring to the boil, stirring continually until the sauce thickens. Cook for 2 to 3 minutes. Remove from the heat and stir in three-quarters of the cheese, the mustard and salt and pepper to taste. Pour the sauce over the cooked chicken, sprinkle with the remaining cheese and brown in a hot oven or under a grill. Serve hot with green vegetables and jacket potatoes. Serves 4.

Devilled Chicken

Grilled chicken breasts stuffed with a curry paste.

4 chicken breasts
2 teaspoons English mustard powder
½ teaspoon salt
½ teaspoon black pepper
½ teaspoon cayenne pepper
½ teaspoon paprika

2 teaspoons curry powder
2 teaspoons French mustard
2 oz butter, softened
1 tablespoon flour
Slices of hot buttered toast
Parsley sprigs to garnish

The chicken breasts should first be baked, with the skin on, until cooked but not browned and then allowed to get cold; remove the skin. Mix the mustard powder together with *half* of each of the salt, black pepper, cayenne pepper and paprika. Stir in the curry powder and French mustard to form a paste. Add *half* the butter and blend together until the mixture is smooth. Make 3 to 4 slits in each chicken breast, and spread the 'devil' mixture into each. Mix the flour together with the remaining salt, black pepper, cayenne pepper and paprika and dust over the breasts. Melt the remaining butter and lightly brush over the breasts. Place the breasts under a hot grill for 5 minutes, turning to brown them on all sides and basting with any juices that form in the pan. Serve at once, garnished with parsley sprigs and accompanied by hot buttered toast, cut into fingers. Serves 4.

Chickenburgers

Round baked cakes of minced chicken.

12 oz raw chicken, minced	**2 oz fresh white breadcrumbs**
1 onion, finely chopped	**Salt and pepper**
1 oz butter or margarine	**1 egg, beaten**

Seasoned flour

Set oven to 425°F or Mark 7. Heat the butter or margarine in a frying pan and fry the onion until golden brown. In a bowl, mix together the minced chicken, breadcrumbs, fried onion and seasoning and bind together with the beaten egg. Divide the mixture into 4 equal portions and mould and flatten into round cakes. Coat well in seasoned flour, arrange in an oven tin and bake near the top of the oven for about 30 minutes. Serve with chips, fried onions rings or baked tomatoes. Serves 4.

Chicken Pie

A simple pie which includes hard boiled eggs and bacon.

1 chicken, or joints, to give
   1½ lb of raw chicken meat
Seasoned flour
2 or 3 rashers of bacon, chopped
2 hard boiled eggs, sliced

1 tablespoon fresh herbs,
   finely chopped or 1 teaspoon
   dried mixed herbs
Salt and pepper
8 oz shortcrust pastry

Set oven to 375°F or Mark 5. Remove the chicken meat from the bones. Put the bones in a pan, cover with water, put on a lid and simmer for 2 to 3 hours to produce some stock. Roll the meat in seasoned flour and put a layer in a pie dish. Cover with the chopped bacon and egg slices. Finish with the remaining chicken. Sprinkle the herbs over the meat and season. Cover with a pastry lid, making a hole in the centre and bake for 1 hour. Reduce the temperature to 350°F or Mark 4 and cook for a further 1 hour. If the pastry appears to be browning too rapidly, protect with a piece of greaseproof paper. Remove from the oven and, through the hole in the pastry, top up with some of the hot stock from the bones, using a small funnel. Serves 4.

Garlic Chicken

Chicken joints coated in garlic butter and crumbled potato crisps and cornflakes.

4 chicken joints	**Good pinch pepper**
3 oz butter	**¼ teaspoon dried thyme**
1–2 cloves of garlic, finely chopped	**2 oz potato crisps, finely crushed**
½ teaspoon salt	**2 oz cornflakes, finely crushed**

Set oven to 375°F or Mark 5. Combine the butter, garlic, salt, pepper and thyme together in a shallow baking dish and put into the oven until the butter is melted. Mix the crumbled potato crisps and cornflakes together on a plate. Dip the chicken joints into the melted butter one at a time, then into the crumbs, coating all over. Arrange the coated joints in an ovenproof dish and sprinkle over the remaining crumbs. Bake in the oven for about 1 hour or until the chicken joints are brown and crisp. Serve with hot boiled rice. Serves 4.

Chicken Chowder

A simple supper dish; a cross between a thick soup and a hot pot.

4 oz cooked chicken, diced	1 pint chicken stock
2 medium onions, sliced	4 medium size potatoes, sliced
1 oz butter	Salt and pepper
1 dessertspoon oil	1 pint milk
1 oz flour	Paprika and chopped parsley to garnish

Heat the butter and oil in a large saucepan and fry the onions until softened. Stir in the flour and cook for 2 to 3 minutes. Gradually stir in the chicken stock, a little at a time, bring to the boil and cook until thickened slightly. Add the potato slices, season and simmer for about 20 minutes until cooked. Add the milk and diced chicken, check the seasoning and cook gently for 10 minutes more until heated right through. Garnish with paprika and chopped parsley and serve hot. Serves 4.

Chicken in Mushroom Sauce

A practical way to cook a chicken which may be too old for successful roasting.

3½ lb to 4 lb chicken
1 onion, quartered
1 large carrot, diced
1 stick celery, diced
3 sprigs of parsley and 1 bayleaf
   tied together with string
6 peppercorns
2 cloves

Salt
A thick slice of lemon (optional)
2 teaspoons vinegar
1 oz butter
1 teaspoon lemon juice
6 oz mushrooms, sliced
2 oz flour
Chopped fresh parsley to garnish

Place the chicken, vegetables, herbs, seasonings and lemon, if desired, in a large saucepan and almost cover with cold water. Add the vinegar and bring to the boil. Cover and simmer for 2 to 2½ hours. Remove the chicken from the liquid and drain well, reserving the chicken stock. Joint the chicken or keep whole, as preferred, place on a heated serving dish and keep warm. Melt the butter in a saucepan, add the lemon juice and the mushrooms and fry lightly. Stir in the flour and fry for a further 2 minutes. Strain the stock and stir into the mushroom mixture a little at a time. Bring to the boil and boil, stirring, for 5 minutes. Pour over the chicken and garnish with parsley. Serve with boiled potatoes, carrots and a green vegetable. Serves 4 to 6.

Chicken and Egg Toasts

A quick way to turn left-over chicken into a light high tea or supper dish.

4-6 oz cooked chicken, finely chopped	**A little milk**
	Salt and pepper
4 rashers streaky bacon	**Slices of hot buttered toast**
1½ oz butter	**Chopped fresh parsley**
4 large eggs	**to garnish**

Pre-heat the grill. Form the bacon rashers into neat rolls, grill until crisp and brown, set aside and keep warm. Meanwhile, melt the butter in a saucepan. Beat the eggs together in a bowl, add a little milk, season and add the chopped chicken. Pour the chicken/egg mixture into the pan and scramble gently until lightly set. Prepare slices of toast, butter liberally while still warm and pile helpings of the scrambled egg on each slice. Top with the bacon rolls and garnish with chopped parsley. Serves 4.

Chicken Pan Pie

A chicken casserole finished with a cheesy crumble topping.

12 oz cooked chicken, diced	1 teaspoon salt
2 oz butter	Pinch of pepper
1 onion, chopped	6 oz cooked rice
2 sticks celery, chopped	¾ pint chicken stock
1 apple, unpeeled, cored and sliced	4 oz hard cheese, grated
1 teaspoon dried marjoram (optional)	2 oz fine white breadcrumbs

Set oven to 375°F or Mark 5. First cook 6 oz rice (see Chicken Kedgeree). Melt the butter in a large frying pan and fry the onion, celery and apple rings until lightly browned. Add the chicken, marjoram (if desired), salt and pepper. Add the cooked rice, pour over the stock and mix thoroughly. Transfer to a casserole dish, cover and cook in the oven for 20 minutes. Take out of the oven, remove the lid and sprinkle the grated cheese and breadcrumbs over the top. Return to the oven, uncovered, and cook for about another 10 minutes until the topping is browned. Serves 4.

Chicken Hot Pot

An all-in-one dish which is made with chicken joints, potatoes, celery and peas; a complete meal.

4 large chicken joints	Pinch fresh ground nutmeg
2 oz butter	Bayleaf
2 onions, thinly sliced	1 tablespoon chopped parsley
6 medium size potatoes, cubed	Salt and black pepper
½ head celery, chopped	½ pint chicken stock
¼ lb mushrooms, sliced	Small packet frozen peas

Set oven to 350°F or Mark 4. Skin the chicken joints and fry them in the butter in a large frying pan until golden brown. Place in a warmed casserole dish. Fry the onions until soft and then add to the pan all the other ingredients except the peas. When everything is heated through pour over the chicken. Bring to the boil, cover, put in the oven and cook for 30 minutes. Add the peas and cook for a further 15 minutes. Serves 4.

Chicken, Leek and Mushroom Pie

Chicken, leeks and mushrooms go well together. If possible, use large flat mushrooms for added flavour.

1 lb cooked chicken, cut into small pieces	½ pint chicken stock
1 oz butter	2 tablespoons dry white wine or sherry
1 medium onion, diced	6 oz flat mushrooms, sliced
1 small leek, chopped	Salt and pepper
1 oz flour	8 oz shortcrust pastry

Set oven to 400°F or Mark 6. Melt the butter in a pan, add the onion and leek and cook gently until soft. Add the flour and cook, stirring, for 3 to 4 minutes. Remove from the heat and gradually stir in the liquids. Return to the heat and bring to the boil, stirring, until the sauce thickens. Add the mushrooms and simmer for 5 minutes. Stir in the chicken pieces and season well. Transfer to a 2 pint pie dish. Roll out the pastry on a lightly floured surface and use to cover the dish. Cut a hole in the pastry lid to allow the steam to escape and bake for approximately 30 minutes until golden brown. Serve hot. Serves 4.

METRIC CONVERSIONS

The weights, measures and oven temperatures used in the preceding recipes can be easily converted to their metric equivalents. The conversions listed below are only approximate, having been rounded up or down as may be appropriate.

Weights

Avoirdupois	Metric
1 oz.	just under 30 grams
4 oz. (¼ lb.)	app. 115 grams
8 oz. (½ lb.)	app. 230 grams
1 lb.	454 grams

Liquid Measures

Imperial	Metric
1 tablespoon (liquid only)	20 millilitres
1 fl. oz.	app. 30 millilitres
1 gill (¼ pt.)	app. 145 millilitres
½ pt.	app. 285 millilitres
1 pt.	app. 570 millilitres
1 qt.	app. 1.140 litres

Oven Temperatures

	°Fahrenheit	Gas Mark	°Celsius
Slow	300	2	150
	325	3	170
Moderate	350	4	180
	375	5	190
	400	6	200
Hot	425	7	220
	450	8	230
	475	9	240

Flour as specified in these recipes refers to Plain flour unless otherwise described.